Pretty Christian

Pretty Christian

Finding perfect faith in an imperfect life

KATIE BARRY

TATE PUBLISHING
AND **ENTERPRISES**, LLC

Published by Tate Publishing & Enterprises, LLC
127 E. Trade Center Terrace | Mustang, Oklahoma 73064 USA
1.888.361.9473 | www.tatepublishing.com

Tate Publishing is committed to excellence in the publishing industry. The company reflects the philosophy established by the founders, based on Psalm 68:11,
"The Lord gave the word and great was the company of those who published it."

Book design copyright © 2014 by Tate Publishing, LLC. All rights reserved.
Cover design by Rodrigo Adolfo
Interior design by Joana Quilantang

Published in the United States of America

ISBN: 978-1-63063-872-6
1. Religion / Christian Life / General
2. Self-Help / Personal Growth / General
14.01.24

Dedication

To Liam and Emily
May He guide your every step and keep you along the way.
Mommy loves you.

Acknowledgments

David—You are my rock. I thank God He knew what He was doing when He created you for me and me for you. There is no one on earth I would rather share this journey with. I love you.

Liam—Thank you for being the best little man, my favorite boy and my one and only Superman. I will stand by you today and always as you continue to grow into the man of God I know you are destined to become. I love you to infinity and beyond.

Emily—You bring unspeakable joy to this world. Never lose that little light of yours. And one day, you will be the prettiest Christian of all. I love you, baby girl.

Mom—Thank you for showing me what it means to sacrifice, to work hard, and to never give up. Without your determination, love, and support, there would be no me. I love you.

Dad—There is no question my passion comes from you. Thank you for instilling in me a drive to succeed, a willingness to learn, and a tendency to care too much. I'll always be your PCK.

Rob—My dear MSF, you are a best friend, a role model, and someone I know I can always run (not walk) to in times of need but also, more importantly, in times of joy. Thank you for always believing in me no matter what.

Brian–I'm not sure you realize it, but you were pretty much my practice kid! Thanks for loving me anyway. Love you. So very proud of you…more than you will ever know.

Aunt Maddy–Thank you for your continual prayers, your honesty (even when I didn't want to hear it), and your undying love for our crazy family. Love, Kip.

Aunt Re and Uncle Gary–We could never repay you for all you have given us; but more than that, the rich spiritual leadership and investment you have made into our lives will never be matched. Thank you for the late-night talks, the roof over our heads, and the love you continue to selflessly share as if we were your own.

Rick, Cindy, and Pete–They say that cousins are your first friends; I say they're the best ones. Thanks for being my friends, my mentors, and my brothers and sister. I wouldn't want to be tortured by anyone else!

Laura–Friends come and go, but sisters are forever. I am so thankful to have you in my life, for forgiveness and for the many new memories to come. Love you.

Michael–Big brother, I see your heart, and I love you for it. Love you more than you know.

Audrey, Teresa, and Brian–There is no such thing as "step." You are my family, and I love you for never being more than a phone call away.

Gram and Aunt Nan–Thank you for being examples of strong, vibrant women who know how to stand their ground! I cherish your place in my life.

Mom and Dad B. and family–Your support has been one of the greatest blessings in my life, and I am so thankful for each of you. Thanks for taking me in. Love you all!

Darla–You are more than a pastor; you are a leader, a mentor, an awesome woman of God, and I am grateful to call you friend. Thank you for always believing in me. Love you much!

Kim–You can't possibly imagine the impact you have made on my life. This book started way back in that catechism class and here I am still writing you notes! Love you.

Nicole–You are my inspiration, and I will never stop loving you or caring too much. You are *Pretty Christian.*

Jenelle–From first friend to friend forever, I will always be by your side. With you, I've had the time of my life!

Christina–Your hilarity and love have gotten me through some of my toughest days, and your friendship takes me through life with a smile.

Jess–You have seen me at my best, and you have seen me at my worst. Thanks for holding my hair, wiping my tears, and sharing so many laughs.

Amanda—I am so thankful to have you in my life today. After all these years, our friendship is one I hold dear and will always treasure.

Sonia—Thank you for encouraging me, pushing me, and laughing at me when I needed it most throughout this process.

FT Ladies—You have my heart. I am blessed beyond measure to count each of you as friends. Thank you for lifting me up, supporting me, and your countless prayers. Love you all!

Debbie–Thank you for helping me believe in myself. For your kindness, patience, honesty, and support, I am forever grateful.

My Lord and Savior—It is all thanks, for, and because of You. I am not worthy, but I am forever humbled by Your grace.

Contents

Foreword

Many years ago, I had the privilege of being a youth leader in our church. It was there that I met a vibrant, beautiful girl who was so full of life that she lit up the room when she entered. As I watched her grow and go through different challenges in her young life, I knew that God had His hand on her life and something very special was in store for her. I remember being at a banquet for our young people where she spoke and gave her testimony as an older teenager. The passion that she spoke with immediately reminded me of what I had felt earlier—God was doing a work within her that would lead her places and cause her to make an impact in her generation.

I didn't see Katie for a few years, but when we reconnected, she poured her heart out and explained the passion that she felt and the impact that she wanted to make in young women's lives. She is a gifted writer and as I read each chapter, I knew that this subject would be groundbreaking to a lot of young women.

This book is powerful and a must read for every young girl growing up in the church. It is riveting and real because it addresses the fact that although we can look pretty on the outside, we need to let God do a real work on the inside of us. Through Katie's own struggles, she lays a foundation that will minister to young people and give them such a hope that God is on our side with His love and protection if we will let Him take control. He is with us even when we struggle at the very core of our being and He is faithful to see who we really are even when we can't see. As you read, know that He wants to uncover His truth and pour unconditional love on you.

—Pastor Darla J. Edlin

Katie Barry

Preface

I'm not a big fan of dirt. In fact, I'm not really much of an outdoor girl at all. So to anyone who knows me, it may come as a surprise that what I am about to share with you evolved out of gardening.

One Friday evening, my pastor made an announcement that she would be hosting a preach-a-thon for our next women's night at church. The opportunity was for women of the congregation to submit a proposal for a three-point sermon. The first seven sermons to be submitted would be reviewed, and if accepted, the women who wrote them would be given the opportunity to share at the next month's women's event.

I immediately knew I wanted to be a part of this awesome night and take advantage of the opportunity to share my heart for young women with the other ladies at church. So I went home and began to think about how I would get all of my thoughts down to just three short points. I thought long and hard, and I prayed long and hard, and nothing seemed to be coming together for me. Until a couple of days later.

One evening, I walked out to my mailbox, and on my way back up the driveway, I noticed that the garden in front of my house was full of weeds. I had just weeded it two weeks ago, but, man, those weeds grew quickly!

So at six o'clock at night, I grabbed my garden gloves and bucket and went at it.

As I began to pull the weeds from my small garden—something my husband and I dug and planted and cared for with our own hands, and were quite proud of, especially since this is not our forte—I began to pray.

"Lord, am I even supposed to do this? What do you want me to say? Maybe I should just forget it. Maybe I'm not meant to be a speaker. I'm a writer. Lord, help me out here."

I continued to weed.

And I noticed something. Some of the weeds were very small and hard to pick out of the dirt. Some were tall—very tall, in fact, for only having grown over two short weeks—and yet could be plucked out even more easily than the baby ones. Others grew out rather than up, and some were mere blades while others had plenty of leaves. But they all had one thing in common—shallow roots.

As I made my way from one end of the garden to the other, I prayed, and I weeded, and I prayed and I weeded. And then I had a revelation: weeds!

The Lord was showing me something in these weeds, and I was finally ready to see it.

Think about weeds for a moment:

- They have shallow roots.
- They grow quickly and easily.
- They appear strong but are truly weak.
- They feed off what is good.

- They spawn more and more weeds.
- They hide among the flowers.
- They can be deceiving.

Where am I going with this?

We have an entire generation of weeds.

What do I mean?

For a long time now, I have felt a heavy burden for our young people—specifically young women. And as I was working in my garden, those weeds quickly began to represent the many girls out there who are more like weeds than the beautiful flowers the Lord has created them to be.

They have shallow roots.

They grow quickly.

They appear strong, but they are weak.

They feed off what is good.

They spawn more and more like them.

They hide among the "flowers."

They can be deceiving.

Here is what I mean:

We have an entire generation of young women who have been raised in the church but have shallow roots. They reach college age, and then we lose them. I know, because I was one of them. They are making poor choices, they are denying their faith, and they are seeking approval from others—from men, from a world of sorrow, hurt, and disappointment. And they are right here in our midst.

Christian women—young women—sit in our pews every week, and they walk out into the world and feel lost. Not because of our God but because of us. We aren't doing enough.

> Though the wicked sprout like weeds and evildoers flourish, they will be destroyed forever.
>
> Psalm 92:7 (NLT)

This world we live in forces our children to grow up too fast. They're objectified, sexified, and glorified at such an early age—by their peers, by their neighbors, by *us*—that by the time they graduate from high school, they think they know it all, have it all, *deserve* it all, and need it all. And why? Because when you have shallow roots—just like those weeds—you sprout up with a false sense of identity. Which leads me to my last point.

They appear strong, but they are weak.

This false sense of identity—of strength and independence that so many young women try to portray—has others convinced, as well as themselves, that they are strong. That they don't need anyone, they don't need us (the church), and they definitely don't need God. To the world, they are independent. To us, they are lost. And why? How did this happen so quickly? Again they have shallow roots.

And just like the weeds, our young women are feeding off this deception and off each other. They think they need to look better, act stronger, and feel superior to the next girl.

Especially those who grow up in the church. These girls are too often overlooked. They are overlooked because we think, well, they're in church, so they are "good." We look at the "un-churched" and somehow believe they need us more, that they will want us more if we can just get a hold of them, but in the meantime, we are losing our own.

Listen carefully, ladies: we need to pay more attention to the weeds.

We need to grab a hold of our young women and strengthen their roots. Plant them in rich soil, fill them with the Word and the Holy Ghost, and send them out so that they don't make the same mistakes we did, so that they don't sprout up quickly, so that they don't spawn more and more like them, so that they are firmly planted in the church on a strong foundation of faith, and so that they rise up as the young women the Lord has created and called them to be.

We don't need any more weeds. We need beautiful, strong, flourishing flowers, and it is up to us to plant the seeds. We have to do more than watch them grow. We have to water them daily! Pluck out the weeds that pop up around them, feed them, and help direct their lives.

> But blessed is the man who trusts me, God, the woman who sticks with God. They're like trees replanted in Eden, putting down roots near the rivers—Never a worry through the hottest of summers, never dropping a leaf, serene and calm through droughts, bearing fresh fruit every season.
>
> Jeremiah 17:7–8 (Message)

If we can get a hold of this and really understand how important this time—the Lord's time—truly is, we will see a generation of young women who won't need to sow their wild oats in college and into their twenties but who will grow into mighty women of God and rise up to be better, stronger, and more beautiful than any generation before. It's their time, and it's up to us to help them grow.

Introduction

No one ever said it was easy. Not life. Not faith. And definitely not being a young woman.

As a little girl with ribbons and curls, your innocence is sweet and your faith is firm. When you become a young woman, that innocence is easily lost, and your faith can be easily shaken. I say this not from judgment but from experience. I have lived in the church, and I have lived in the world. I have struggled to be better, and I have worked hard to be worse. I have sought the Lord, and I have hidden from Him. But in the end, with Him is where I long to be, and because of His grace, I am blessed.

There is nothing you can do to make Him stop loving you. There is nothing you can say to make Him leave you. There is nothing—not one thing—you can do that will change His desire to give you all that He has for you. But you can make decisions that will leave you feeling alone (though you never are), forgotten (though you never will be), and destined for disgrace (though all He has for you is good).

We've all been told what's right, what's wrong, what pleases God, and what doesn't. Yet for some reason, we make bad choices, we take the wrong path, and we do so knowing that what we do is far from good. So why do we do it? Why is it so difficult to be the perfect picture of innocence and purity when we know what it takes? Why is it so hard for us to simply be the young women the Lord wants us to be, the young women we *want* to be?

How many times have you felt like you are nothing? Nothing without your friends; nothing without your boyfriend; nothing without your Guess jeans, your Coach bag, your monthly pedicures, or your new car. We have all been there. We have all had moments, or even lifetimes, of feeling like without something or someone we treasure most in our lives, we somehow fall short. You may be thinking that's ridiculous; that you know your clothes, your possessions, or even your loved ones aren't more important than God. We like to say—and often convince ourselves—that we don't value material things as much as we do, or that we don't place our loved ones before God. But we do.

As a little girl, I feared my mother. It was a healthy fear (to obey and to be careful not to disappoint), yet I feared her and arguably placed her above my fear of God. Of course, it may sound absurd to think a little girl might have the wherewithal to consciously place her mother, or anything for that matter, above the Lord, but there comes a point in all our lives, some sooner than later, when we knowingly decide what we will do, what we will not do, and why we choose to do or not do those things.

As I grew older, there were times that I focused my attention on the Lord, but there were more times when I did not. My focus went to things like friends, boyfriends, jobs, school (yes, even school!), and sometimes anything but God. We all run at times. We all hide at times. But He never does.

We can't be so self-absorbed to think that God cares that much about us, can we? Yes. It's a divine paradox that my menial brain may not ever quite master, but here is my attempt: we must know without hesitation that God loves us so much that He cares about all that we do, all that we are, and all that He wants us to be.

God loves you. He cares. He is always there. He wants more for and from your life. He wants you to love Him, trust Him, fear Him, and honor Him. He wants you to grow in Him, to flourish and spread His love in a way that only you can do. But in order to do these things, you have to follow His Word. It's not always easy, it's not always fun, but in the end, it will always lead you to where you need to be—the best possible place for you, determined by Him.

What the Lord has for you is better than any fairy tale you can imagine because His love for you is the greatest love story of all. His idea of your perfect life is the very definition of perfection, and He wants nothing less for you than all that He has predestined for you to have. But you have to take it. You have to receive it. You have to trust in Him and Him alone.

I struggle with expressing to others—especially young women—how blessed I am because I fear they might look at me and think, *Well, hey, she turned out all right! I'll be just fine. Someday I'll be happy. Someday I'll fulfill my destiny. Someday it is all going to work out the way it is supposed to.*

But will it?

I was always the "pretty" Christian. I loved the Lord, I was on fire for God, and I was actively involved in my church. I survived much of high school unscathed by sex, drugs, or falling into the traps of the world. But slowly, things changed.

Slowly I realized that the stuff I had been avoiding my entire life looked kind of fun. Slowly I made one small decision after another that led me down a path, from taking one sip of alcohol to eventually ending up in a ditch on the side of the road. From a high school boyfriend to dating guy after guy in college, my purity had been compromised, and I lost sight of what I had once so desperately tried to protect. My life—seemingly overnight—went from the pretty Christian to pretty messed up. And I didn't even know it was happening.

I never abandoned my faith, but you would have never known who I was in the Lord if you saw me on a Friday night. I had become lukewarm in my faith and gotten caught up in the ways of the world. I was no longer a pretty Christian girl but a young woman who was only pretty Christian.

Have you ever heard testimonies of people who find Jesus and, from that point on, go on to be preachers, missionaries, etc.? People who come from abusive childhoods, have converted from other religions, or have lived drug-induced, hate-filled, crime-infested lives suddenly become saved and turn their lives around on the spot—do you ever envy those people? I do.

I don't mean to imply that I envy their pain, but I do envy their revelation of the love of Jesus Christ. How awesome to never know about the Lord, and then all of a sudden, you meet Him and your life is forever changed. Yet so many of us grow up in Christian homes, maybe attend Christian schools, go to Christian churches, and hang out with Christian friends, and we are lukewarm when it comes to our relationship with Christ. But why? We know the same God we love and serve is the same God who saves the abused, the afflicted, the addicted, and the accused. He is the God who gave His only begotten son so that our sins could be forgiven. Yet as Christians we ignore Him. We get bored with Him. And sadly, we sometimes turn so far away from Him that we forget He is even there.

Growing up in the church is a wonderfully difficult thing. As a child, your innocence is sweet and your faith is strong. But as you grow and mature, you are faced with decisions and a harsh reality that isn't as comfortable as the life you live within the four walls of the church you call home. And when you are a developing young woman, it can become increasingly difficult to navigate your life, your love, and your faith, no matter who you are.

It doesn't take a single moment in time or a particular action to become lukewarm in our relationships with the Lord. It takes days, weeks, months, and sometimes years to slowly but surely become so complacent, so spoiled that we forget just how much we need Him in our lives. We don't understand that we are nothing without Him. We are only something because of Him, and He will never leave us.

I have overcome. I have been blessed. But what if I never had the chance? What if those mistakes I made were more than just mistakes? What if they brought pain and suffering far beyond anything I or you could imagine? What if they brought death to me or, worse, to someone else? I have been in situations that should have ended differently. I have made decisions that should have resulted in nothing less than disaster. Yet I am here, and I believe I am here for a reason.

You may not have the same opportunities that I have or as many chances as I have seemingly been given. I believe the Lord's grace—and only by His grace—is why I am here today, to share with you, to relate to you, and to let you know that only He can save us from ourselves.

I don't ever want a single young woman (or anyone for that matter!) to look at my life and the blessings I have been given and think, "She turned out okay, so I will too." Instead, I want you to look at my life and say, "I don't want to make the same mistakes she did." I want you to say, "I don't want to take the chance of not making it through."

I will not tell you that I am not ashamed of my past or that I don't have regrets. I will not boast about the things I have done as though they don't matter. In fact, it's just the opposite. I am embarrassed. I am repentant. And I am in awe of what the Lord has done for me.

Understand that I believe my testimony is not one to emulate but one to fear. Don't think for one minute that you will be okay. Trust only in Him, seek His face, and know that you are nothing without Him.

This isn't an autobiography, nor do I expect you to be interested in my life story; but I do share these things because through my experiences, the Lord has revealed things to me that I would otherwise never see.

For example, I know the love of a father times two. I know firsthand the struggles of a single mom, because I was raised by one for the first decade of my life. I know what it's like to be the youngest child, the oldest child, the only child, and the middle child. I know what it's like to love someone who struggles with addiction, and to help family during times of need, and to feel like giving up. I know what it's like to have an overflowing pantry, and I understand how it feels to have to eat mayonnaise sandwiches because you have no food. You see, through it all, through all of the hurt and pain, joy and laughter, life and love, the Lord has predestined every aspect of my life and has revealed to me an amazing lesson every step of the way.

That's what I want you to take away from this book: that even in your darkest hour or happiest place, the Lord is at work. No matter what you are going through, He can turn it around. And I know because He has done it for me, and He can and will do it for you.

This is *Pretty Christian*.

I Heart You

Above all else, guard your heart, for everything you do flows from it.

Proverbs 4:23 (NIV)

The heart is a funny thing. We sing about it, we give credence to it, and we even use it to replace the word *love* either by symbol or by name. And why? Why is the heart—a rather disgusting-looking organ in reality—idealized to be something so lovely, so beautiful, and so important as love?

I'll tell you why: the Lord gave us a heart in order for us to seek after His love. Our brains function in logic and assist in the carrying out of our free will. But our hearts—our hearts are the very place our life flows out of. Our hearts beat, and therefore, we live. If we live, we are able to seek God, and God *is* love. So our hearts beat because of love, out of love, and for love.

I don't want to get too philosophical here, but just think about all the ways in which we use *heart* to replace the most important aspects of our lives, even beyond love. We speak of athletes who play with heart (determination). We speak of leaders who lead with their heart (passion). We even talk about our hearts breaking when we experience hurt or disappointment. See, the heart is more than just an organ. It is a

God-given gift that is at the very core of who and what we are. The heart is the most important physical manifestation of God's love for us because with it, we have life, and therefore, we have love.

Everything you do—from the breath you make to the steps you take—flows from your heart.

So if our hearts are so important, so essential to who and what we are, then why do we give them away so freely? It's easy to talk about hearts and love and have images of pink and purple valentines in our minds, but let's take this idea of the heart to another level.

Your heart is not something that comes with a key. It doesn't come in a box, and it is not made of glass. But you do need to protect it.

For just a moment, I want to strip away all of the idealism, all of the romanticism, and all of the images of chubby little babies with wings and puffy arrows from this idea of the heart. Let's even forget about the images of brokenness and shattered hearts we so often see. Imagery can be really effective when driving home a point, but for this one, we need to forget what we already know.

In order to understand God's heart, we must first understand our own.

So let's be real for a moment: hearts cannot be broken, except in death. So long as your heart beats, you live. Therefore, your heart is never broken so long as you live.

It nearly brings me to tears to think of how we have trivialized the heart in such a way that has led us, especially young women, to believe that it is something that is so worthless, so breakable, and so easily fixed or even replaced. The truth is that your heart should be your most prized possession because it gives you life, and you only have one.

Yet so often, many of us give it away.

Think about your favorite doll growing up, and think about how devastated you would have been if someone had taken it from you and ripped its head off or destroyed it beyond repair. I vividly remember one doll that my mother had given to me for Christmas when I was only a year old. It was a precious baby doll dressed as a clown with bright orange, curly hair. I loved that doll. My mother had given it to me; it was special to her, and it was very special to me.

During one particular playdate when I was about ten years old, I had invited a number of friends to come over on a Saturday afternoon. We all ventured to the basement where there was a makeshift play area. (In other words, the basement was unfinished, and this was the corner of the rather dark and dismal space that housed boxes and bins of my toys.)

At one point, things seemed to be going very nicely. I was pleased that all my little girlfriends were getting along and everyone was playing separately but together. A couple of girls were pretending to be ballerinas at the ballet barre my grandfather had made for me; another friend and I were drawing on my school-sized chalkboard; and then there was Elizabeth.

It was as if time suddenly began moving in slow motion and everything around me went black—except for her.

"What are you *doing*?" I dropped my chalk, leapt over an old wooden-box-turned-Barbie-tote, and lunged at my "friend."

Elizabeth was, for all intents and purposes, doing what any normal ten-year-old girl might do: she was brushing a doll's hair. But not just any doll. It was *my* doll. My precious curly-haired, carrot-colored-haired clown was now a frizz-headed bozo with patches of missing locks, thanks to the tangles that had gotten caught in the plastic-toothed brush.

That little girl had no idea what hit her. I snatched the doll, grabbed the brush, and yelled through my tears, "Why would you do that!"

Poor Elizabeth. She didn't mean any harm. How was she to know how special that little clown was to me? After all, aren't dolls made to be played with? (That's a loaded question for a kid like me who organized Barbie clothes rather than dressed up the actual dolls. But my OCD is for another discussion.)

As you can imagine, that playdate came to an abrupt end. My mother gave me a knowing look and a tender pat on the back. As we said good-bye to Elizabeth and the rest of the girls that day, I knew my dolly would never be the same. I knew my friend didn't mean to do anything wrong or hurtful, but the reality was, she did, and the damage was done.

So what would you do if you allowed someone to take something very precious to you only to break it? Would you fix it? Would you buy a new one? What if it was something irreplaceable? You obviously wouldn't let it break on purpose. You would never give it away willingly if you knew someone was going to hurt it. After all, it's special to you. It's one of a kind. It's yours and yours to protect.

What if we felt that way about our hearts? What if we were so jealously protective over the one and only heart the Lord has given us that we seemed utterly unwilling to let anyone near it, let alone give it away, unless we knew beyond a shadow of a doubt that they would handle it with care? What if we truly understood that, just like our favorite doll, once our heart "breaks," it will never be the same?

The truth of the matter is, once something is broken, it is never "as good as new." Even if it appears perfectly repaired to the naked eye, as though nothing had ever brought damage to its exterior at all, you know it has suffered a break.

Have you ever heard the saying "Hearts were made to be broken"? I am here to tell you that's a lie. Hearts were *not* made to be broken. They were made to bring life. They were made to love. They can't be glued back together, and they don't magically fix themselves. They may get banged up, bruised, and sometimes even disregarded, but they can only be truly healed by the one and only Great Physician.

Only the Lord can mend a broken heart because your heart is only His to mend. Don't give your heart away. The Lord is asking you to protect it and to keep it safe. And if you take anything away from this book, take away the fact that your heart isn't yours to give. It belongs to the Lord. He has lent it to you so that you might live and love, and it is your responsibility to guard your heart because "everything you do flows from it" (Proverbs 4:23, NIV).

Of course we can't always be certain that others will handle our hearts with care. But we can be mindful to not carelessly give our heart away without first seeking wisdom from the one who made it.

Remember, a heart is only broken in death, and the Lord wants you to live. Just as a mother may hand down a special something to her daughter in hopes she will keep it with great care, so the one and only Father asks that you guard your heart, for He has fashioned it to bring life.

Best Friends Forever

Little girls dream big and play hard. They fantasize about the future and try to soak up the present. They long to be older and yet delight in their youth. And at the heart of it all, what they really want is to be loved. Little girls want to be loved in their yesterdays, todays, and forevers. They dream of promises everlasting and visualize twinkling stars and glittery dresses. Why? Because what it all means, especially by the world's standards, is that we are loved. The hope of Prince Charming? Based on love. The idea that we will someday ride off into the sunset? Love. The thought of having children? They'll love us too. And maybe even a dream of being successful or even famous? Love. Love. Love.

All we want is love. Even from our girlfriends.

We love our friends. We hate our friends. We laugh with them. We cry with them. We talk to each other. We talk about each other. It's just such a twisted, confusing, comforting, loving, dramatic ball of an emotional mess, yet as women, we just can't get enough.

We all have friends—whether they start as neighbors, classmates, or cousins—and we quickly learn that our girlfriends can be a great source of strength in our lives.

Friendship, especially between women, is a beautiful thing. And when it is true, loyalty is at its core and longevity will be its fruit.

Over the course of my life, I have made a lot of friends and I have lost a lot of friends, but the friends I keep are the ones who build me up. I have some old friends, some new friends, some lost and some found, but if I count you as a friend, I cherish your place in my life.

Three Musketeers

I am blessed with some amazing women in my life and a number of beautiful friendships that I cherish greatly. And while I value all my girlfriends, there are two that are my oldest and closest friends. It is through these friendships that I have learned some of life's most valuable lessons, and looking back, I am able to see God's grace.

Meet Jenelle and Christina.

Jenelle

When I was five years old, Jenelle and I became friends in Ms. Bliss's kindergarten class. We went to school together, danced together, and our mothers were very much alike (both single moms from similar backgrounds). We seemed to basically be cut from the same Italian-American cloth. I am sure you had or even still have a childhood friend who fits into this mold—one who looks like you, acts like you, and even smells like you (or your mom's cooking, at least).

So on paper, we were perfect friends. But in reality, we were actually quite different, and those differences only became more apparent as we grew older.

After kindergarten, Jenelle and I got separated. She continued to go to the school where we met while I was enrolled in a private school when my mother moved us from the suburbs to an apartment in the city. (Moving was something I did so often that I eventually lost count, but in my adulthood, I recognize this as a major contributing factor to the woman I am today.)

Although Jenelle and I ended up attending different schools, our mothers helped us maintain our friendship by scheduling playdates and sleepovers on a fairly regular basis. They even enrolled us at a new dance school together. After only three short years of being apart, we were brought back together in the same classroom at the same school for the fourth grade. I was elated!

The cool thing (for me, anyway) was that Jenelle and I not only were back together but also were both new girls at this school. Even Jenelle had transferred to this particular public school due to a move. My mom and I were back in the suburbs, thanks to her new marriage, and I was on my way to stability. At least for a little while.

As the days and weeks passed and the school year was well underway, Jenelle and I became less like besties and more like frenemies. My oldest friendship was becoming my newest disappointment, and my nine-year-old brain couldn't quite cope with the loss of what I once thought so ideal.

When my supposed best friend was having more fun with other people, or was telling me she was annoyed with my phone calls, or was not sitting with me at lunch, my little-girl heart was proverbially broken (but I didn't know then what I know now).

I loved her. Why didn't she love me?

Now, every relationship has its ups and downs, and friendships between little girls are certainly of no exception. My best friend at age five remains one of my best friends at age thirty, but not without a price. You see, over twenty-five years of friendship with one woman, I have learned something about love: It's not about how many fights you have. It's about how many times you are willing to make up. It's not about how often you get together. It's about how you spend your time when you do.

That's how I understand things now, not how I saw things then.

During that fourth-grade year, I had a very difficult time understanding that even though Jenelle showed her love differently, she still loved me. In my eyes, she was not nearly as loyal or as loving to me as I was to her. After all, if she was really my friend, she wouldn't have had that other girl sleep over and not include me, and she definitely would not have sat with someone else at lunch. All of that was my perception.

But here was the reality: her loyalty wasn't weaker—it was different. She didn't need to be attached to my side to know my heart, or even to know her own. She knew I was her friend, and that was all she needed. She didn't question my love for her or where or how I spent my time. She knew we were friends, that we would stay friends, and nothing or no one would ever get in the way of that. But I needed more.

Neither Jenelle nor I were wrong in the way we approached our friendship. We were just too young and immature to understand what the other needed. She needed a bit more space. I needed a little more attention.

That's kind of how I imagine our relationship with Jesus sometimes. We know He's there, we know He loves us, but we don't always spend the time with Him that He so badly wants and deserves. It doesn't mean we don't love Him or that we don't need Him in our lives. But maybe we should consider His feelings a little more often. He loves us in spite of our ability to ignore Him, pass Him by, or choose others over Him. He loves us in spite of our faults, and He never gives up on us, even when it seems as though we really don't care.

But we do care. So often we take for granted the fact that we know He will never leave us and that He loves us more than we know. Just as Jenelle knew I would never *not* be her friend, we know Jesus will never *not* be our Father. And just as I was jealous for my friend—because I loved her, wanted to spend more time with her, and needed her in my life—Jesus is jealous for us.

Exodus 20:4—5 (NKJV) says, "You shall not make for yourself a carved image—any likeness *of anything* that *is* in heaven above, or that *is* in the earth beneath, or that *is* in the water under the earth; you shall not bow down to them nor serve them. For I, the LORD your God, *am* a jealous God, visiting the iniquity of the fathers upon the children to the third and fourth *generations* of those who hate Me,"

He knows we love Him, but He always longs for more. More of our time, more of our hearts, and more of us is what

He desires. As Christians we tend to do just enough to let Him know we love Him. We go to church, we pray before meals, and we even cry out to Him in times of need. But we also, more often than not, push Him aside, especially when we seem to be presented a better offer.

For Jenelle, her better offer sometimes came in the way of new friends. But I never left her. I may have been hurt at times, I may have been frustrated, and I may have even temporarily walked away from our friendship a time or two. But I never gave up.

God never gives up, no matter how many times we push Him to the side.

Christina

My first encounter with Christina was rather awkward. I was cast as Princess Jasmine in our school's production of *Aladdin* and in desperate need of a Jasmine-esque costume (parachute pants and a belly shirt—a very popular ensemble in 1992). Christina, an avid dancer and owner of many bedazzled apparel options, offered her eclectic wardrobe to the chorus director in order to outfit the cast for our concert.

I distinctly remember being told by our director that she had secured a costume for me and that I was to pick it up from a girl named Christina out by the bus loop after school. In a drive-by-drop-off kind of approach, Chris walked passed me as she ran to her bus and threw—yes, *threw*—the clear plastic costume bag at me, complete with the red-and-gold costume balled up inside.

Thanks?

I wore the costume for the show, gave it back, and that was that.

We didn't become friends until the following year, when our two classes shared teachers for math and English. We quickly realized how much we had in common, including Jenelle. The three of us formed a friendship that would prove unbreakable over the years, but not without trial.

Once we reached middle school, Christina and I grew really close. She was a strong friend, one I knew I could rely on, and she proved her loyalty time and time again. Though many around us were against me, Christina was always by my side (bullying may be a modern-day buzzword, but it is an age-old problem). She protected me, she defended me, and she even laughed in the face of those who tried to attack me.

My favorite story in the history of our friendship is the time she literally laughed so hard in the face of a bully that they fled the scene, crying. Really! In the eighth grade, Christina and I had lockers that were very close to each other in the same hallway. Toward the end of passing time one day (the 3.5 minutes you get to leave one class, go to your locker, and head to another), a couple of bullies walked up behind me and tapped me on my shoulder. One was the bully, and one was sort of a bully coach. What do I mean by *bully coach*? Well, there was a girl playing the bully and another girl literally whispering in her ear, coaching her with things (mostly expletives) to say to me.

As the bully paused, waiting to be fed her next line, Christina jumped in from out of nowhere and, while laughing, yelled out, "Who are you?" I couldn't help but laugh right along with her at this point because the scenario was really *that* ridiculous. We didn't even know who these girls were!

At the time, I took this sort of thing very seriously. I was faced with constant confrontation because of a specific group of girls who loved to spread rumors and lies about me, and I ended most days in tears. I spent my entire middle school career in fear, petrified of the girls around me and the things they would say. I was always looking over my shoulder, wondering what was going to happen next or who would be waiting around the corner. So for me to be laughing in this case was truly extraordinary.

I can't really remember what happened next, but I do know the rest of the confrontation was short-lived. I learned in that moment that someone loved me enough to stand by my side—to laugh with me, to cry with me, and yes, to even chase away the enemy.

The absurdity of it all helped break the fear I had been living with for so long. It actually ended up being a major turning point in my life because in that pivotal moment, I learned that a true friend—a best friend—was defined by what had just happened. Love, loyalty, and laughter.

Christina was and is a best friend to me.

Knowing Who We Are

When we least expect it, the Lord shows up to simply remind us He is there, just like when Christina showed up for me that day in eighth grade. He is by our side, and He is our greatest defender. When the enemy shows up, Jesus is already there. Sometimes we don't even need to ask. He simply loves us that much.

See, the bullies of the world only act as mere puppets for the true enemies of our lives. When we stand up and take authority (even with laughter), the enemy must flee!

> For we are not fighting against flesh-and-blood enemies, but against evil rulers and authorities of the unseen world, against mighty powers in this dark world, and against evil spirits in the heavenly places.
>
> Ephesians 6:12 (NLT)

What I didn't realize while I was being bullied throughout my adolescent years was that all of the attacks, all of the confrontations, and all of the inexplicable hatred that was being thrown my way had purpose. At the time, no one understood why so many of my peers hated me, including me.

People would often ask, "Why do they hate you?" And I would always reply with, "I don't know!" To which they would undoubtedly respond, "You must have done *something*, Kate."

And so began a cycle of internal questioning that I have struggled with for years:

Why did they hate me?

What did I do?

What did I say?

Why don't people seem to understand me?

And forget other people taking my word for it. I started to doubt myself. Maybe I was delusional to think that I truly had done nothing wrong. If so many other girls hated me with such passion, I must have done something. Right?

Wrong.

I wish I could have seen then what I see now. The truth is that there was never an explanation in the natural because the fight existed in the spiritual. I was a baby in my relationship with the Lord back then, having only been (truly) saved at the age of twelve—but that's when it all began.

The minute I said yes to Jesus was the minute the devil said, "Game on." The problem was not that the enemy didn't know who he was messing with. The real problem was that I didn't know who I was. I didn't understand the authority I had. I had no idea about all of the gifts the Lord had given me and the many blessings that He had in store. I had only just begun my walk with Christ, and the devil was on high alert. It wasn't enough to have gone to church since birth. That didn't put the devil into action. My will to dedicate my life to the Lord—my small yes—started him on the move.

It's no wonder my girlfriends didn't jump ship long ago, but two decades later, they are still by my side. We had no way of knowing what was to come over our teens and twenties, and now into our thirties, but what I do know is that the friendships we share are some of my greatest gifts.

For more than twenty-five years, Jenelle and Christina have remained to be constant sources of love and support for me, and I hope I have done the same for them. We've laughed together. We've cried. We've loved and we've lost. But most importantly, we've grown and never grown apart.

Though there have been times when we've gone our separate ways, each of us have always known the other two were there. We never leave. We never forget. And we always show up. We can go days, weeks, or even months without talking, and when we reconnect, it's like no time has passed at all.

And so it goes for your relationship with the Lord. He is always there, no matter how far you stray. When you come running, He will pick up right where you left off, because He truly is your one and only BFF.

Father Figure

So many of us are blessed to know the love of a father, but too many are not. It's common today for young women (and young men) to grow up in homes that are lacking true examples of what a father should be. For me, I was and am fortunate to have multiple father figures in my life, all of whom have helped me appreciate my true Father all the more. But it hasn't always been that way.

My parents separated when I was only two and divorced before I was three. My father moved to Virginia shortly thereafter, and I spent the rest of my childhood living with my mom. Even though my dad lived in another state, he returned home frequently, and I spent time with him on holidays and during the weekends when he was in town. We had a good relationship, but not one where we chatted over breakfast or ate dinner together every night. That's just the unfortunate reality of having a parent who lives out of state.

My father—a hardworking, very successful businessman—was not around to discipline me, but he was careful to keep me in line as best he could from afar. He may not have been around to hug me every morning or tuck me in at night, but I knew he loved me and I knew he was only a phone call away.

My father and I didn't truly have a traditional father-daughter relationship until I grew much older. As I matured, I spoke with him more and more frequently, and by the time I was in college, we became much closer than we had been during my adolescent years. I began to see just how much we were alike, how this man I spent relatively little time with as a small child had helped shape who I was, and how much it meant to me to please him. To this day, others point out (and my dad and I laugh about) how incredibly alike we are. It really is remarkable, given the distance between us as I was growing up, but our commonalities (as well as our differences) have helped form a bond between my dad and me that is very special.

While my father and I didn't share the same house, I was fortunate enough to have a stepfather who loved me unconditionally as if I were his own. He and my mother began dating when I was only five years old, and they were married three years later. Rob (my stepfather) was a young, caring man with a heart of gold when he entered my life. He was ever present and playful and was a constant source of comfort in my life. He was careful to never assume the role of father (as in an authority figure, a disciplinarian, etc.) but was very much a dad. He allowed my mother to make the big decisions—discipline, boundaries, and even rewards—and provided a positive male figure for me as I grew up. He was and remains to be a very important part of my life.

By all means, my "less than traditional but far from extraordinary" upbringing was a recipe for disaster. My life had all of the ingredients to create some major daddy issues due to the confusion that could and should have come from being a product of divorce—an epidemic among far too many young women (and men) today. That is not to place blame or point fingers at my parents; their marriage may have failed but their love for me was always evident. Divorce is never pretty, but one thing I always knew and still know is that I was and am loved.

Unfortunately, I come from a family where divorce runs rampant, and for reasons far too complicated to get into here, I continually sought approval for fear of rejection in all areas of my life (I even struggle with this battle in my adulthood, but again, that's for a later chapter). Until recently, I thought that maybe my myriad of insecurities stemmed from not having a "traditional" or "normal" home: you know, the kind with a mom, a dad, 2.5 kids (from the same two parents), and a white picket fence.

But why—if I, in fact, had so many positive role models in my life—did I long believe my life should have ended up in disaster? Well, thanks largely in part to the wonderful men who helped raise me, my life did, in fact, turn out okay. And for that, I am thankful. Despite where my life could have ended up, I am married to a wonderful husband and father whose main priority is to be there for his family. But I haven't always been smart enough to let the positive male influences in my life translate well into other areas, including my faith.

Let me explain.

While I was blessed enough to have more than one dad, I was also surrounded by other male figures who helped shaped my life; from grandfathers, uncles, and cousins to big and little half-brothers and a stepbrother, my life has never lacked quality examples of good men. Yet each of these men couldn't be more different, and each affected me in his own way. Especially my grandfathers.

Grandpa Dominic

My mother's family was always very close, especially during my childhood, and we spent a lot of time together. A lot. (Some would argue too much!) Both of my mother's sisters had also been divorced, and so the three sisters and their four collective children became one big, loud, crazy, loving family. We even all lived together in a two-bedroom apartment at one point—imagine the fun *that* was!

My maternal grandparents were the overarching heads of the family. Lena (Vincenza), my grandmother was short and portly and the sweetest little Sicilian lady with a big heart and an even bigger appetite. My grandfather, Dominic, was an old-school Italian rebel who had met the Lord later in life. He was generous and gentle, but the scars of his past haunted him and often physically hindered him from being the jovial, affectionate grandpa I know he so wanted to be.

Having suffered a severe, life-threatening accident during his last years as a city firefighter, my grandpa was stricken with a number of diseases, including diabetes and scleroderma, and we have often wondered if he lived with additional neurological disorders and bouts of depression. His physical ailments often translated into what can only be described as a surly disposition, but not all the time. In fact, most of the time he was lovely...and loved.

I'll never forget the contradictory love and simultaneous fear my grandfather evoked in me as a small child. He was not a very large man, but his presence could fill any room. He was relatively short in stature and slight in weight, but his voice could bellow far beyond the four walls of his tiny, little ranch-style home. Yet he was also warm and caring and remarkably emotional in his own way.

I spent a lot of time with my grandparents, and most of my summers were spent in front of their TV. My grandmother would cook for me morning, noon, and night, and she loved to wait on me hand and foot. (Eventually her love of food became my love of eating and—as my stepfather used to say—I became "pleasantly plump" between the ages of nine and ten. Once I gave up the pudding pops and the five-course meals three times a day, I was back to less plump and more pleasant by the time I reached the fifth grade. It was a difficult but delicious year.) I still love the smell of coffee and scrambled eggs in the morning because it immediately draws me back to being five years old, watching *Sharon, Lois, and Bram's Elephant Show* while sitting with the TV tray entirely too close to the screen.

During those days, I didn't see too much of my grandfather; he was always working in the garage. He loved to build things, even when the scleroderma had hardened his hands to the point where they were barely useable any longer; he continued to find ways to saw, drill, build, and create. But sometimes he would find his way into the living room and say to me, "Hey, Charlie"—he called me Charlie because he could never get anyone's name right, and for some reason, that one stuck—"wanna go for a walk?" To which I would inevitably reply, "No thanks, Grandpa." Frustrated at my lack of ambition, he'd say, "Oh, come on!" Again I'd refuse the offer, and he would undoubtedly walk out of the room, shaking his head. I disappointed him.

His efforts to spend time with me had failed. I should have gone with him. He was only trying to help. I should have known that this was his way of loving me. But I didn't. I didn't know until it was too late.

Too often I've treated my Heavenly Father the same way. He's asked to spend time with me, and I've declined. He's made me offers, which I have turned down. He's extended his hand, and I have pushed it away. And just like my grandpa Dominic, He continued to seek me out even when He knew He would be rejected.

The good news is, unlike our earthly fathers (or grandfathers), our Heavenly Father will never give up. It is never too late, and He will never leave. No matter how many times you say no, no matter how often He asks and you turn away, He will continue to love you, to ask you to spend time with Him, and to desire to have more and more of your heart regardless of how hardened it has become.

My grandfather passed away when I was in the eighth grade. He died only eleven short months after we lost my grandmother. He loved her, he missed her, and he simply could not live without her. And I was left full of regret.

I have often mourned the fact that I didn't take him up on all of those offers. I regret not spending more time with him, asking more questions about who he was, where he'd come from, and all that he knew. And mostly, I regret that he may have left this earth not knowing the profound impact he had on my life.

As a woman, I am thankful for his strong example of what a strong man of God can be (did I mention he joined the rodeo as a teenager and later the navy, and fought in World War II?).

As a mother, I am thankful for his example of discipline and forgiveness.

As a daughter, I am thankful for his desire to spend time with me and to show me love.

As a wife, I am thankful for his example of love for my grandmother and his ability to bring our family together.

If I could thank him today, I would. I would tell him that through his life—his example, his hard work, his triumphs, and his failures—I am able to see my Father's love. I think that would make him proud.

Grandpa Bernie

Right after college, I held a job as a marketing writer for nearly a year, but I was quickly faced with an opportunity to work for our local county legislature—something that both intrigued and excited me as I had found myself interested in politics since I was old enough to understand the importance of right and wrong, black and white, Republican and Democrat, conservative and liberal.

What's remarkable about my affinity for all things political was that although it was very much a part of my father's life and his family's history, I did not spend much time with them to have expected their beliefs and convictions to resound so loudly in my life as well. My father was (and is) extremely politically astute, and his father and grandfather played roles in local politics from the time they found themselves in the United States. (Both sides of my family emigrated from Italy to upstate New York in the early 1900s, which makes me Italian American through and through. And also adds to my love of food!)

My dad, while not a politician by trade, has always been involved in the political world. His father, my grandpa Bernie, worked in our local-county office building for many years. And lo and behold, I found myself working—where else?— in the local-county office building at the age of twenty-three.

When my grandpa learned of my new position and where I would be working, he was beaming with pride. It was as if this man, whom I hadn't really spent much time with or gotten to know as a child, suddenly came to life and also suddenly became more than relevant within mine.

I began to realize that my grandfather was not just an old man who helped bring me into this world, but he was also a man with a rich history, and his legacy was one that contributed to my destiny. From the moment we shared the county office building as common ground, my grandpa Bernie and I grew closer with each year until his death just six short years later. I watched his health slowly decline as he suffered from dementia. He would recount the same stories over and over about my grandmother and their courtship, their lives together and his undying love for her. And just after we had truly begun to get to know each other, my grandfather passed away.

So where's the lesson? It lies in the unknown, the underappreciated, and the selfishness that led me to believe I was my own person rather than be appreciative of all those who had gone before me to pave the way for my life, my love, my work, and my future.

Not only was it cool that my grandfather had spent so much of his career in the same place I was living out the early years of mine, but it was amazing he had worked closely with a man that would one day become my father-in-law. My grandfather started a title company, and when my father-in-law was starting out as a young attorney; his specialty was real estate law. They formed a friendship and shared many business transactions, friendships, and common ground. And the moment my grandfather learned whom I was dating and would eventually marry, he was thrilled. He had loved my father-in-law more than thirty-five years prior, and now his granddaughter would be marrying this honorable man's eldest son.

It seemed as though the hand of God could not have been more present in my life. It had been pieced together so meticulously, and my grandfather was an integral part.

How often does our own arrogance get in the way of recognizing all that the Lord has done to bring us to where we are? Our successes and our failures are not merely our own but are pieces of a much greater plan—the Master's plan—both thanks to and in spite of ourselves. And how amazing is it to experience the revelation that someone and/or something that has been a part of your life all along was an even greater part than you ever knew or cared to find out? This revelation is both thrilling and depressing for me. It's thrilling because I stand in complete and total awe of God's ability to piece things together in such a miraculous and merciful way. Yet it's depressing because it took me more than twenty-three years to realize and appreciate someone who had helped make me who I am.

What the Lord has helped me see through this incredible example of what some might call coincidence is that He is the one who holds my life in the palm of His hand. He is the one who picked me, called me, blessed me, and entrusted me with great gifts. And why? Because His purpose for my life is much more than anything I can imagine. While so many people have played critical roles in my life (both good and bad), I am just one small piece of so many others.

Isn't it awesome to think that God uses each and every one of us? He uses us to help others; he allows us to hurt, to be hurt, to succeed, and to fail all for His greater good. I don't know about you, but for me, this is an awe-inspiring revelation that I am so very thankful for. And it's all thanks to the love of our Father.

Katie Barry

All of the men in my life have helped shape who I am as a woman, but not in the way the enemy would have had it. If it were up to him, I could have resented my father for not being there (even though he was and is and always will be). I could have resented the fact that my mother remarried (even though my stepfather is a wonderful man whom I cherish and respect). I could have ended up marrying a man like my grandfather, who was cold on the surface and full of secrets to take to the grave (even though his heart was full of goodness, mercy, and love). Or I could have ended up never knowing the love of a man who appreciates the woman God has called me to be (like each and every father figure I have been blessed to have in my life).

Over the years, I have sought attention that I already had but chose to ignore. All too often, I looked past the blessings and focused on the curse. I have, at times, resented the bad and overlooked the good. And all along, God was doing His great and mighty work in me, to me, and through me. Sure, I could have ended up in a bad marriage. I come from a broken home. And sure, I could have been another statistic—a teen mom, a college dropout, a divorcee, or an adulterer. But I am none of those things, which is thanks and due to the grace and mercy of the One I call Father. He is my salvation. He is my peace. And only He has made a way where the world has said there should have been no way.

He has protected me, secured me, and kept His Word. Because He is my one true Father.

What I would have every one of my earthly father figures know is this: I am so incredibly blessed by them. I have had the opportunity to learn from them, to share with them, and even to disagree with them. And yes, I count our disagreements as blessings because it is through those times that I have been able to grow.

I have grown into the woman I am today—wife, mother, daughter, sister, cousin, niece, and friend—because of and thanks in part to the impact of the wonderful men in my life.

We all have to realize (especially as young women) that no matter what our relationships look like with our fathers here on earth, every relationship (or lack thereof) happens to us and for us for a reason. The Lord's purpose may not always be visible, but it is always there.

Our earthly fathers are to be honored and respected no matter what their roles have been in our lives. But our Heavenly Father? He is the only one who will never fail us. He wants what is best for us, expects the best from us, and has the best plan for our lives. He is the ultimate father, and He, dear sisters, will never let us down.

I am thankful to be His.

Katie Barry

Love, Honor, Respect, and Obey

There's nothing worse than feeling like you don't have a purpose—at home, at work, with family, with friends, or even in life. Purpose is an important piece of who we are and what we do, yet sometimes it's hard to recognize. It can be hard to uncover and it can be difficult to follow, but I assure you, it's always there.

We don't always understand our purpose as it relates to others. Sure, we all have purpose in our lives, but what is your purpose, say, in your relationship with your mother? Yes, of course you are to honor her, respect her, and (hopefully) love her, but what is your purpose as it relates to her? And what is her purpose in your life?

Mothers and daughters have long shared emotionally charged relationships full of passion, love, sorrow, and joy. They can be beautiful pictures of honor and respect, or they can evoke horrifying feelings of hurt and pain. But for most of us, our relationships are a little bit of everything all wrapped up into one big ball of emotional mess: mostly love, some hurt, a lot of misunderstanding, but in the end, we share an unbreakable bond with our mothers that is unlike any other relationship we share on earth. Our mothers give us life.

It's no secret that mothers and daughters fight, especially mothers and teenage daughters. And why is that? Why, when we reach a particular age, do we have a revelation as to just how misunderstood we are and how stupid our mothers can be? Well, we aren't always misunderstood, and they aren't always stupid. In fact, it's quite the opposite. But somewhere, somehow, at some point along the way, mothers and daughters go from best friends to worst enemies, and it can seem to happen overnight.

So often we hear from women who say it wasn't until they were married and had children of their own that they truly understood why their mothers did/said/acted the way that they did. But that doesn't exactly help when you're in the middle of an epic mother-daughter battle at the age of sixteen, does it?

What can be done so that we might understand our purpose as it relates to our mothers? I have often wondered—and wonder—exactly what my purpose is as it relates to my relationship with my own mom. Am I supposed to fulfill the dreams she had for herself? Am I supposed to make her proud? Am I supposed to show her I am my own woman or help her to see I am the woman she has helped me to be? The answer, while it may surprise you, is none of the above. The answer is wrapped up in understanding the rest of the story; it's about recognizing her place in my life and my place in hers.

Because I Said So!

There were never four words I hated to hear more than when my mother would say, "Because I said so!" It was even worse when she would say, "Because I am your *mother*, and I said so!" But now that I am a mom, I can relate—sort of.

Any mother will tell you that what she asks of her child has purpose. In other words, just because she doesn't continue with "And my reason is…" doesn't mean there is no purpose behind her request.

Think of it this way: Do you have a curfew? Or can you remember a time when you did? Let's say, for example, that your mother tells you to be home no later than 9:00 p.m. on any given night. Your response to her might be "But why, Mom?" to which your mother would reply (say it with me now), "Because I said so!" However, what your mother isn't saying is that she wants you home by 9:00 p.m. because she is concerned about your safety. She is instilling responsibility and accountability while expecting you to act out of obedience. To you, your mother is being unfair and unyielding. But to your mother, her mere request should be reason enough alone.

The problem is, she isn't explaining, and you aren't reading between the lines. Should she explain? Well, not necessarily. She is expecting that you will *love* her enough to listen, *honor* her enough to heed her request, *respect* her enough not to ask why, and *obey* her because of her position of authority over your life.

This, my sweet sisters, is a battle all too commonly fought and far too often lost by both sides. And why is it lost? Because mothers often fail to explain, and daughters often fail to listen. Although daunting and sometimes arguably unnecessary, it is critically important that children understand the why just as much as they know and understand the how. But equally as important, children must also understand that sometimes the why is simply because they are loved.

Whether you are a teenage daughter experiencing this struggle today or an adult woman being reminded of your mother-daughter struggles of the past, or even a mom who is dealing with struggles from the opposite side, what we all must realize is that these struggles most often come from one place—love.

My mom practically invented "Because I said so," and I hated it. I still hate it. But now, I get it. "Because I said so" isn't code for "I am determined to make your life miserable." It can most often best be translated into something more along the lines of "I love you and need you to respect my wishes because I have good reason for what I ask of you."

Now, don't go home to your mother (if you still live with her) and expect her to all of a sudden start making her requests in this way! I can't be responsible for that. But my goal is to help you understand that whether you are walking in a similar situation today or are remembering your mother-daughter battles of days past, you will begin to see the why of your mother's requests and hopefully start to understand her purpose in your life.

As a mother, I now find myself making a conscious effort to offer explanations to my children. Something in me vividly remembers just wanting to know why, so I am determined to help my children understand why I make certain—not all—requests of them. My heart's desire is to see them obey with a joyful heart, not because they always love what I ask of them but because they understand that what I ask of them is always out of love. And while my four-year-old son hasn't quite yet mastered the complex concepts of *why* or *how* or even *because*, he does respond when I kneel down, hold his chubby little cheeks in my hands, and tell him, "Mommy will never ask you to do something just because I feel like it. Everything I do is because I love you." And that really is reason enough. It may not be much better than "Because I said so," but it makes me feel a heck of a lot better, and someday, I hope it makes him feel better too.

Our Heavenly Father asks the same of us: to do as He has requested simply because He says so. And so often we respond with "Why, God?" But what if we didn't? What if we always acted out of obedience, disregarding the why and being thankful for the who, the what, and the how?

> You shall walk in all the ways which the LORD your God has commanded you, that you may live and that it may be well with you, and that you may prolong your days in the land which you shall possess.
>
> Deuteronomy 5:33 (NKJV)

Being obedient brings blessing! God doesn't ask anything of us simply because He can; He only requires of us what is good, and it's always out of love.

In John 14:15 (ESV), Jesus says, "If you love me, you will keep my commandments." The same is true of our parents. If we love them, we must obey them, and it is through our obedience that we show our love.

Now, let's be clear—our parents aren't perfect and they are certainly not always right, but it is not our job to always ask why. It is our job as daughters, of both our earthly parents and our Heavenly Father, to obey.

Of course, there may be instances when parents' requests are inappropriate, maybe unrealistic, impossible to fulfill, or unhealthy to obey. It is in these instances that your willingness to do what is right and good and safe must take precedence. This is when the Word should be your guide.

The purpose of every daughter is to love, honor, respect, and obey. And when we cannot love or respect, we must still honor and obey. I used to have an extremely difficult time with that. What exactly does it mean to "honor thy father and thy mother"? Are we to honor them as in bow before them? No. Are we to honor them as in place them on a pedestal? No. Are we to honor them as in accept them for who they are and their position of authority over our lives? Yes.

We are to honor our parents—our human, sinful, imperfect, misunderstood, and misunderstanding parents—and when we do, we glorify God.

Please don't misunderstand; this isn't always easy. In fact, for some it may never be easy. But honoring your parents, particularly during the most trying times, is what God calls His daughters to do. And He asks this of us out of love.

So then, what is your purpose as it relates to your mother? I can't answer that for you. But what I can tell you is this: your purpose in life includes the mother the Lord has chosen for you. For me, my mother was my one constant in life. No matter where we lived or moved to, no matter which school I ended up at any given year, or no matter who my friends were at the time, my mom was my home. In some ways, she still is. I realize, though, that not everyone has that in a mother. For some, your mother was merely the vessel to bring you into this world, and therefore, your purpose was helped birth by her. For others, your mother has been a constant source of love, support, and friendship, and she has encouraged you along the way. But no matter what your relationship with your mother has been like or still is, you are always called to love, honor, respect, and obey. And when you do, you please the Lord.

Give and Take

I love to give. In fact, I love to give much more than I like to receive. I know it sounds trite and cliché and possibly a bit contrived, but I kid you not; I have a heart to give, and it brings me more joy than you can imagine.

When I say *give*, what is it that comes to mind? Do you think about large boxes wrapped in pretty paper and topped with extravagant bows? Do you think of a tiny little box with a shiny surprise inside? Do you think of money? Or, on the contrary, do you feel suffocated at the thought of giving anything away?

For me, it brings me joy to make other people happy; unfortunately, it has sometimes been to my own detriment. Let me explain.

Just the other day, I was in my bathroom getting ready for a typical summer afternoon. I reached for my toothbrush and toothpaste and noticed that my husband had squeezed the tube from the middle (again), so I took a moment to force the toothpaste to the end of the tube (as it should be); this truly is an example of OCD at its finest. Anyway, after I brushed my teeth, I dried the brush by squeezing it in my towel (because putting away a wet toothbrush would get the basket in the drawer all wet, and then bacteria would grow; we can't have that [again, OCD]). While doing this, I was reminded of a season during my single days where I took in a friend in need.

Friends No More

The circumstance that brought my friend to live with me was ugly; she was in an abusive relationship and living in squalor, and although we were not much more than acquaintances at the time, I decided it was up to me to rescue her. So after listening to her cry one last time about how her live-in boyfriend mistreated her, I told her to hop in my car, and we went straight to her apartment to get her things. She was going to move in with me, and I would not take no for an answer. We collected everything we could fit into my SUV and would worry about the rest later.

During her first evening in my small-yet-roomy one-bedroom apartment, I gave my new roommate a little lesson on how to properly clean the sink after brushing her teeth (oh yeah, I was a real joy). I specifically showed her how "great" it was to squeeze the toothpaste all the way to the end of the tube every time you brush (because it's that much less work at the end!) and how to properly dry your toothbrush to avoid a mess (if you're making a face in disgust at my ridiculous requirements right now, imagine how my poor friend felt). I instructed her with a huge smile plastered across my face, believing that she would be grateful for my amazingly helpful tips!

Despite my insanely neurotic demands, my friend lived with me, rent-free, for just a couple of short months before my lease would end. It's safe to say that our friendship did not survive. You can't imagine why, right? Well, shockingly, it had little to do with my OCD and more to do with pride, expectations, and overzealous generosity.

What's that, you ask? Well, I probably would have denied it at the time, but helping out my friend did more for me than it did for her. While I was nothing short of a mess myself, opportunities to help others such as this allowed me to feel better about what I was doing, how I was living my life, and excusing my bad behavior by doing "good" for others. If I'm being honest, I got much more out of the situation than she did, I am sure. In fact, I am pretty sure she walked away from that entire time and thought I was (1) crazy and (2) a complete disaster in my own right. She was right on both counts.

Out of that experience, I learned a valuable lesson: when we are determined to give, we sometimes focus on our own feelings rather than those of whom we are trying to help. Of course, I believe my friend was grateful that I allowed her to stay with me and helped her leave behind a potentially disastrous situation; but I don't think she was prepared to feel like my charity case, nor did she want to be treated like a child.

This story, this memory, came flooding back to me before I could twist the top of the toothpaste tube all the way closed. "Lord, why am I remembering this now?"

It suddenly became so clear: I know how to give. Sometimes, that's all I know how to do, and so I panic. I react. I give, give, give until I suffocate those to whom I am giving, and before I know it, I have depleted my own supply. I am great at giving, but what I don't know how to do is receive. I know how to fill others up. I know how to work hard to make others happy. Yet I don't do the same for myself.

For years (for most of my life, really), I have been so consumed with making others happy—whether it was to make them like me, respect me, accept me, or simply not hate me—that I have taught myself to give as a way to gain approval. As much as my giving is about other people, it's more so about me.

That hurts. It hurts because, as I explained in the beginning of this chapter, I *love* to give. But if I listen to what the Lord is telling me today, as an adult woman trying desperately to learn and grow and help others do the same, He is showing me how my giving has hurt me in the process.

It may seem convoluted and twisted and confused, but the reality is this: my giving doesn't have to change. My ability to receive does.

Blessed Is She Who Gives

> Each one must give as he has decided in his heart, not reluctantly or under compulsion, for God loves a cheerful giver.
>
> 2 Corinthians 9:7 (ESV)

So it's safe to say that our giving delights the Lord.

In Luke 6:38 (ESV), we are instructed to give in order to receive:

> Give, and it will be given to you. Good measure, pressed down, shaken together, running over, will be put into your lap. For with the measure you use it will be measured back to you.

And in Acts 20:35 (NKJV), Jesus Himself said that "it is more blessed to give than to receive."

It's All About Me

Throughout my life, I have given away my heart, my body, my mind, and my soul. I have given away money, clothes, furniture, and shoes. I have given away time, energy, work, a listening ear and a shoulder to cry on. And all the while, I have been depleting myself of all that the Lord continues to give to me.

That is not to say that I have not given with a joyful heart, because I have and I do. But what the Lord is showing me today, in this season of my life, is that because I have the heart of a giver, I have too often placed that need, that urge, that desire to give (or to please other people) above my own needs. And in doing so, I have caused my own pain by placing unrealistic expectations upon others, upon relationships, and especially upon myself.

Can you relate? Do you enjoy giving, even to your own detriment? It has taken me thirty-plus years to recognize that, but I believe the Lord is showing me these things today to bring healing to me and to you.

As givers, we are blessed. But we must also be willing to receive. We give out of our own needs to feel loved, accepted, appreciated, and adored. We give to boost others' perceptions of us, to prove to ourselves, and to force our own ideas of thankfulness upon others.

For me, as much as I can clearly see just how my giving has often been about me and the deep wounds that I carry, I have struggled to receive. From gifts to compliments to affection, I give a lot but try desperately not to take. Let me rephrase that: I do not feel comfortable when I receive; therefore, I feel as though I do not show just how much I truly appreciate what others give to me. I somehow feel ill-equipped to express my sincere gratitude so instead I have missed opportunities to be blessed.

But I ultimately had to ask myself this question: how can I continue to give if I don't allow myself to receive? We can only give so much before we have to fill back up; in other words, we can't give what we don't have.

Deceptive Denial

In my early twenties, I spent three years in an on-again-off-again relationship that was anything but healthy, godly, or good. What I thought I learned through that relationship (back then) was that in order to truly be in love, we must be willing to love without expectation. I believed that true love meant loving someone without ever needing to feel loved in return. I had convinced myself that this must be what true love really was; I didn't need him to love me back—or so I thought. And not only did I think this was true love, I convinced myself that I had been enlightened! I had this revelation that true love was always about the other person. Yes! That true love must mean when you care so much about someone else that you completely deplete, ignore, and neglect yourself. (Sounds awesome, right?)

And that's exactly how the enemy works. The lies and deception that I began to both tell myself and believe were suffocating my spirit, and it was all because I wanted to *give* love. I had this need to please, to give whatever someone else wanted at any cost because I had been so convinced that I no longer mattered.

I shudder at that thought today not because I was wrong but because I was so sure that I was right.

The truth—God's truth—is that love is His greatest gift. To love and be loved is woven into the very fabric of the character of God; God is love. So what would make us think that we should not have access to love, especially since it is the very essence of all that He is? And even worse, how could we be so deceived to think that we, as children of God, do not deserve love?

The Bible teaches us that "every good gift" is from the Lord: "Every good gift and every perfect gift is from above, coming down from the Father of lights with whom there is no variation or shadow due to change" (James 1:17, ESV). If every good gift is from Him, how or why would we ever not want to receive with open arms? It would seem as though that if we reject a good or perfect gift, be it tangible or not, we are truly rejecting the Lord.

Whoa.

Am I suggesting that every time we reject a gift that we are really rejecting the Lord? Well, if it is good (like love or care, a financial blessing, a gift given out of love, etc.) then yes, I am suggesting that our ability to receive must be intimately interwoven with our ability to recognize what we are receiving as coming directly from the Lord. Now, if what we are being given or offered is bad, if it comes from someone or something unholy or that is displeasing to God, then we have an obligation to reject that so-called gift. If we truly understood the Lord's love for us and that "every good and perfect gift" comes from above, then maybe, just maybe, we would have an easier time accepting the gifts that others have to give. Maybe, just maybe, if we value ourselves as much as the Lord values us as His children, then we might just be able to receive with a cheerful heart so that we may be able to continue to give in the same way.

This is as much a revelation to me as it hopefully is to you. If you are in a relationship where you love and give and love but never receive love in return, get out. That's not what the Lord has for you. And more importantly, that is not what He wants for you. He has so much more if you will only walk away from the pain and receive the love He has waiting for you. It may not be today, it may not be tomorrow, but if you surrender to His will for your life, and your love, you will find happiness beyond your wildest dreams.

Fill 'Er Up!

If you are someone who simply loves to give but has a difficult time receiving, start accepting the positive gifts others bring to you as a way to fill back up. It can be as simple as a hug or as elaborate as a piece of jewelry, or it can be something intangible, like a compliment. Whatever it is, start learning to receive. It's okay! It's a wonderful thing when others pour into your life, and you have to give yourself permission to receive them.

Picture for a moment an empty bucket; now, imagine filling that bucket with water and handing it to your best friend. Your friend accepts the bucket, and before she can even put it to good use, she dumps it on another friend standing next to her. Wait a minute, right? You *just* handed this bucket of water to your friend, and while you didn't offer instructions, you trusted she would put it to good use. She could have watered her garden; she could have taken a drink from it or cooled off on a hot summer day. Instead, she quickly and carelessly dumped all of that precious water onto someone else! She then turns to you holding her bucket, waiting for you to fill it back up.

Well, that doesn't seem right, now does it?

Yet that's what we do with the Lord!

Think about it. He fills us up, and we ask for more. Some of us even give it all away before we have a chance to appreciate what we've been given. And then, to make matters worse, we turn right back around and say, "Okay, God, fill 'er up!" Of course He wants us to share. Of course He calls us to give. But He is also looking for us to slow down, accept, and appreciate His gifts to us, and stop throwing it all away—even when we do so with the best of intentions.

This can be said for material things as well as spiritual. If God has blessed you, be a blessing to others, but not without thanking Him first. And most importantly, don't expect to keep getting filled if you never take the time to say thank you and appreciate what you have been given.

Do you see what I am saying here? We can only give away what is ours in the first place. What is ours comes from the Lord, and so we must learn to enjoy being filled as much as we enjoy giving away. In the same way, we must enjoy giving as much as we enjoy being filled.

> But someone who does not know, and then does something wrong, will be punished only lightly. When someone has been given much, much will be required in return; and when someone has been entrusted with much, even more will be required.
>
> Luke 12:48 (NLT)

Maybe you enjoy receiving more than you enjoy giving. In that case, you have to learn to give before you can ever get filled up. And if you simply hang on to what's been given to you without ever blessing others, your bucket of water becomes stagnant and stale. You need fresh water! And you can only get that when you share what you've been given.

These lessons aren't easy, and as I said in the beginning of this chapter, I struggle with these things today. Just because I like to give doesn't make me a better person than those who like to receive. In fact, I wish I could be more like them and truly show my appreciation to others and to the Lord in ways that somehow feel "good enough." However, what we all have to see and understand is that there must be balance—that in our giving, we must also receive, and when we receive, we must be willing to give.

Now *that's* a lesson in love!

Ultimately, giving is not about money or material things; it's about helping one another, showing care and concern, and offering gifts—tangible and otherwise—as a way to express our love and the love of our Father. Continue to give, but be just as willing to receive, and when you do, you will find you will never run out of love—for you or anyone else.

Relationship Ransom

How can you identify a healthy relationship from one that is costing you too much? Whether it's a friend who always reminds you of the time they bought you lunch, a family member who no longer speaks to you because they don't feel appreciated enough, or a coworker who feels they should have received the promotion instead of you, some people will simply never be satisfied with who you are or what you do. And you have to know that that's okay.

What about when *we* are the ones who place a ransom on our relationships? Of course, some relationships in our lives are unhealthy because of someone else. But sometimes, we are to blame.

Friendly Lunch Turned Costly Meal

No cash? No problem. Say you are out to lunch with a friend and realize you don't have any cash in your wallet. Rather than letting you take money out of an ATM and spend an extra five dollars in fees, your friend offers to foot the bill.

"Don't worry about it," she says. "It's on me!"

You let her know she doesn't have to do that, but she insists. So, you finally give in and thank her over and over. "Thank you so much! I'll pick up the tab next time."

And you do, without hesitation. You gladly return the favor the next time around and are more than happy to do it. Who doesn't love helping out a friend, right? The problem is, not everyone "helps" for free.

That lunch gains interest over time, and before you know it, it eventually costs you more than a lunch in return. It costs you your relationship. How? Your friend didn't give to you freely. Her generosity came with a price. For whatever reason—be it jealousy, resentment, or misplaced anger—she felt that you owed her more than a thank-you and a return favor. It's inexplicable because truly, if you knew what would have let her know how much her kindness meant to you, you would have done that very thing. But here is what you need to understand: she likely doesn't know either.

Sometimes (more often than we like to know or admit) people take issue with us. One day they are our friend, the next they are our enemy, and all the while our heads are spinning as we try to figure out what happened.

Has this ever happened to you? Are you nodding your head knowingly, wishing this scenario didn't sound so familiar? And now are you waiting for an earth-shattering explanation as to why your gratitude was not enough? Stop. You will most likely never get one. And here is the hardest thing to swallow: you will not be free of the hurt until you stop needing an answer. Cut your losses and focus on the friendships that build you up free of charge rather than those that weigh you down with guilt and resentment. The bottom line is that some people, for various reasons, will sometimes choose to walk out of our lives. What you have to know is that it is not always on you. Sometimes it's on them.

You know the old cartoons where the woodpecker ever so lightly taps his beak on the desert floor, and within seconds, one single peck causes a small crack that then turns into a bigger and bigger fracture and eventually the entire earth separates? The ground shakes, the earth crumbles, and all of a sudden, the woodpecker is left standing miles away from his enemy on another piece of land, separated by a gaping valley. Now, slow that progression down a bit, and you have the reality of how one small crack in a relationship—especially with a close friend or within a family—can bring forth life-changing separation.

How does this happen? Well, it often starts out quite small. Just as in the example with the friend who bought your lunch, expectations take over and people end up getting hurt by others who may never have intended to cause any pain at all. In families, these hurts can too often be easily found; someone says something at a birthday party that they thought was in jest, but the person it was directed toward doesn't find it funny. Or maybe your sister told you she didn't like the shoes you had on last weekend. Maybe your brother told you his friends thought you looked fat in your bathing suit.

We can sometimes laugh these things off on the surface, but what lies beneath is a small hairline crack on the ground of our soul. It may not be big, and it may go unnoticed for days, weeks, months, or even years, but eventually that crack can become a break—and that break can bring forth an earthquake. Do you know what I am talking about?

I would guess that you have been hurt by a family member more than once in your life. Who hasn't? It's what you do with that hurt that will make the difference in your life. See, your sister, your brother, your cousin, your aunt, or your uncle may not know they have hurt you. Should they be more sensitive to your feelings? Maybe. Should they not tell the truth in an effort to spare your feelings? Maybe not. But what they can't possibly know is how deep a small crack can go if it goes unnoticed. They can't know your pain if you never share it with them, and if you internalize it, it will only continue to grow.

You can only let others hurt you if you give them permission to do so. Listen, we all internalize hurt sometimes. But you have to be willing to nip it in the bud rather than let it blossom into an ugly garden of bitterness and sorrow. Tell your sister she hurt your feelings before you tally up all her comments into a bill too large for her to ever repay. Let your brother know what he said was inappropriate instead of charging him for his behavior for the rest of your life. You just never know how much pain you can save yourself if you are honest and upfront about your feelings, especially with those whom you love.

No, you are not always wrong for feeling hurt. No, people should not be able to walk all over you. But you have the power to either let it in or keep it out.

> "Trust in the Lord with all your heart and lean not on your own understanding; in all your ways submit to Him and He will make your paths straight."

> Proverbs 3:5–6 (NIV)

You may be hurting, you may get offended from time to time, but rather than let the hurt seep in, give it up to God. Don't try to figure things out on your own, including how or why others hurt you. Instead, ask the Lord for the best way to address the ones you love, letting them know what they say or do has meaning. Only He can take away the sharp sting of someone else's tongue, and only you can give Him permission to do so.

Coworker Competition

You will often find that no matter where you work or what industry you are working in, there will always be some level of competition among your peers. Without competition, no one would ever get ahead. Competition is good. It's healthy. But it can definitely get ugly.

In one job that I held early on in my career, I was particularly happy with my work. I enjoyed what I did, and my performance reflected it. When the position of second-in-command became available, I was elated. I thought I was more than just a shoo-in for the job; I was convinced that they *had* to give it to me. Not because they owed it to me, but because I worked hard, I was good at my job, and they knew how badly I wanted it. I had worked in that particular position for a couple of years at that point, and seniority should have counted for something—or so I thought. On top of it all, I was a woman and my boss was a man. Therefore, it made the most sense that his counterpart would be a woman—you know, to balance out the department. It was all settled in my mind.

In reality, that was not what happened at all. If you are thinking I got passed over, you are wrong. What could be worse, you ask? Being ignored. That's right. I was not just passed over, I was *completely* ignored. The position that had been vacated was not filled. It was not eliminated, it was left empty. Rather than fill it with me or anyone else, they simply chose to leave the position vacant. I kept waiting and waiting for the phone to ring. I expected them to call me any day to tell me I could pack up my things and move to the office next door. But the phone never rang.

Eventually, I left that job. I would be lying if I didn't admit that this situation had something to do with it. It did. However, it was a small piece to a much larger puzzle of hurt and resentment that I would have to deal with in my own heart, on my own time.

Some months later—over a year, in fact—I attended an event with my husband, and many of my former coworkers were there as well. One man whom I had been very fond of (he was a big teddy bear kind of guy) came up and gave me a big hug. "Katie! It is so great to see you! Guess what? They just promoted me, and I couldn't be happier! Isn't that great?"

His smile couldn't have been any bigger, and my ego couldn't have taken a bigger blow. *How did he get that job? He hasn't put in enough time! He didn't work as hard as I did! He's not a woman! How did this happen?*

The poor guy had no idea why I basically gave him a half smile and went on my way; no congratulations. No high five or big hug. I just smiled and walked away. I have seen him a few times since that fateful night, and he still seems uneasy around me. I think it's because he thinks I dislike him or that he did something to offend me but wasn't quite sure what it was. The truth is, he didn't do anything wrong. It was just easier for me to dislike him than to admit I didn't get what I wanted or what I thought I rightly deserved.

It wasn't his fault. In fact, he didn't even get the promotion *over* me. I wasn't even employed in the same office when he was promoted. So why did it upset me so much?

To this day, I don't feel I have the right words to explain just how hurt I was by this scenario. It wasn't my former coworker's fault. It wasn't even the employer's fault. It was mine. It was my hurt that I allowed to fester deep within my heart. And the fact of the matter is, I had no reason to take it out on him.

How many times have you misdirected your hurt or your anger toward someone who didn't deserve it? How many times have you allowed yourself to get upset over something that was never intended to hurt you? We do this so often, or at least I do, and yet we are surprised when others do it to us.

My advice? Don't get caught up in the competition of life. It's not just in the workplace that we fight for positions and titles. We compete day in and day out with those whom we love the most. We compete with people we don't even know. We compete with ourselves, all for the glory and for the reassurance that we are good enough.

Can I encourage you to stop? Stop competing. Stop charging others. Stop paying the debts that have already been paid.

Relationships are difficult; they can be costly, but they don't have to be. They can be rewarding but aren't always. And they can be genuine, beautiful, and helpful. Remember to treat others as you would like to be treated. It's a commandment, after all: "Love your neighbor as yourself. There is no commandment greater" (Mark 12:31, NIV).

God knows what He is doing. Trust in Him and leave your relationships in His hands. He will show you those that count but aren't costly, and He will show you those to invest in and those to set free. If you seek Him first, the rest will fall into place.

Beautiful Mess

You're beautiful from head to toe, my dear love, beautiful beyond compare, absolutely flawless.

Song of Solomon 4:7 (Message)

As you well know, young women—Christian or not—are inundated with the importance of safe sex, birth control, and the power of no. We are told to embrace our sexuality yet be responsible about doing so. We are shown images of supermodel "Angels" walking down runways in scantily clad lingerie (which is supposedly socially acceptable) and then shunned by the church for wanting to look and feel pretty and, dare we admit, sexy.

The mixed messages are nearly impossible to weed through, and yet somehow, we are supposed to understand the weight of pregnancy and motherhood in a world that shuns the end but glorifies the means. In plain English? We are taught to love sex but to hate the consequences.

The world wants us to live and breathe sex. It's everywhere. It sells. It's what seems to make the world go round. But the church wants us to ignore it—hate it even—until we are married, of course. Then we are supposed to love it.

Huh? It's no wonder we're confused!

We try to make sense of two points of view that couldn't be more opposite, and for some reason, there seems to be nothing in between, which is where most of us lie, especially as teenage girls. We want to be pure. We want to do what is right. But we also want to be loved. We want to feel pretty. We *want* to be *wanted.*

There has to be a better way. There has to be a better way for us—for you—to feel all of those things without compromising what we know to be right and good. There has to be a way to be pretty *and* Christian without being pretty Christian.

So what does that look like? Well, it's not "safe sex." Safe sex is the world's answer to embracing your femininity and your womanhood while protecting yourself against STDs and unwanted pregnancies. But what is "safe sex", exactly? Isn't it really all about dodging bullets? And it certainly doesn't help you dodge the spiritual bullets that come along with it. Sure, condoms and contraceptives are ways to help avoid diseases and babies, but there is something more that transpires when a man and woman physically connect. More than bodily fluids get mixed up when two people literally become one. But are we supposed to just ignore that too?

The proof is in the severe emotional distress that so often accompanies premarital sex. The tears, the obsessing, the heartbreak, and the pain that go along with having multiple partners is nothing short of tragic, yet so many young women (and men) don't know a life without it.

Nothing about having sex is "safe" when it is done outside of God's will. And God's will is for a husband and wife to become one. Then and only then is sex ever truly safe because then and only then is it in line with God's will.

Listen, this idea of purity is nothing new, and I am sure you have heard it all before. Whether you are perfectly pure or far from perfect, one fact remains: when it comes to sex, God's Word is black-and-white.

> Let marriage be held in honor among all, and let the marriage bed be undefiled, for God will judge the sexually immoral and adulterous.
>
> Hebrews 13:4 (ESV)

> Flee from sexual immorality. Every other sin a person commits is outside the body, but the sexually immoral person sins against his own body. Or do you not know that your body is a temple of the Holy Spirit within you, whom you have from God? You are not your own, for you were bought with a price. So glorify God in your body.
>
> 1 Corinthians 6:18–20 (ESV)

You are not your own.

It is critical that we glorify God with all that we are and all that we have, and being a sexually immoral or seductive woman (or man) far from pleases the Lord. Again His Word is clear:

> "For the lips of an immoral woman are as sweet as honey, and her mouth is smoother than oil. But in

the end she is as bitter as poison, as dangerous as a double-edged sword. Her feet go down to death; her steps lead straight to the grave. For she cares nothing about the path to life. She staggers down a crooked trail and doesn't realize it."

Proverbs 5:3–6 (NLT)

That last line really strikes me: "She staggers down a crooked trail and doesn't realize it." It strikes me because it was me. I staggered down a crooked trail, and I didn't even know it. I didn't realize the destruction I was bringing into my own life—to my body, my spirit, my soul—by staggering down a path that was anything but straight and narrow.

It's not that I didn't know right from wrong, pure from impure, or good from bad. I did then just as much as I do now. But I didn't realize how destructive my choices and my actions would be because I refused to pay attention. I was having too much fun ignoring my conscience (and the voice of the Lord) to care about what the consequences may or may not be. I didn't end up pregnant, and I didn't end up sick. I didn't end up broken, abused, or permanently damaged. But I did end up lonely, hurt, and in a lot of pain.

What I refused to see then was that I was more than just defying God's law; I was knowingly refusing to accept what was good. I was more than just making choices that were less than holy; I was laughing in the face of the Father who created me for a divine purpose and plan. I was sowing things I would never want to reap. But I did it anyway.

Do It Anyway

When I was a little girl, my Aunt Ria had a saying: "We'll do it anyway!" Whenever she wanted to take me somewhere fun—like the circus or the zoo—and my mom would say no, Aunt Ria's response was, without fail, "We'll do it anyway!" When Aunt Ria wanted to give me ice cream or cookies before dinner and my mom said no, Aunt Ria's response? "We'll do it anyway!" That was just her way, and I (of course) loved it. She was fun and exciting. She was always willing to go on an adventure, and she never hesitated to take me along.

Now, her defiance was fun. It was funny, it was lighthearted, and her intentions were good. But for my mother, it was nothing short of annoying. Still, although she didn't necessarily follow the rules, my mom would usually let it slide because she always knew I would be okay.

My mother could only say no so many times before she knew her no would eventually have to turn into a yes. Those yeses didn't necessarily mean she condoned what we were doing; she didn't. But she knew I would come home, and she knew that if I got sick from too much sugar, got scared of the lions and tigers and clowns, or came home full of dirt, mud, and muck that she could then explain to me that her no only turned into a yes to teach me a lesson. And many a lesson did I learn.

Sometimes I wonder if the Lord allows us to make mistakes in the same way. "Go ahead," He says. "But when you return, you'll understand why I said no." That's not to say He condones our behavior, our actions, or our choices. It just says He has given us free will.

> The heart of man plans his way, but the Lord establishes his steps.
>
> Proverbs 16:9 (ESV)

My mother never wanted me to get sick or hurt or scared. But she knew if I did, she could then teach me why it is important to listen to her. The Lord never intended for me to live a life of destruction, even if it was for a short while. But He can (and is!) use that season as a teaching tool to illustrate His grace, mercy, and love. He has used every single mistake, every bad decision, every wrong choice, and every misstep to glorify Him by turning every test into my testimony. He has made me whole (though I was damaged), He has provided for me (though I should be alone), and He has healed me (though I suffered through a lot of pain). He has made a way in spite of my "crooked trail," and He has forgiven my every sin.

I am not suggesting that God somehow wanted me to do all the wrong that I have done in order to use me, but I am suggesting that He (and only He) can use those things for good. What we mess up only He can fix, and sometimes, our beautiful mess becomes a part of His perfect plan.

Thank God for that.

Empty

For I know the plans I have for you," declares the LORD,
"plans to prosper you and not to harm you, plans to give
you hope and a future.

Jeremiah 29:11 (NIV)

You never know just how empty you can feel until you have,
at one time, been full. Think about a brand-new coffee
mug—do you see it as empty? Or is it simply ready to be
filled? What about after you've used it for the first time? That
moment when you've taken your last sip of a cup of coffee,
tea, or hot chocolate but haven't yet filled it again—in that
moment, your cup feels empty. You drank from it. What was
once there is now gone. But it isn't quite clean, and it has yet
to be filled again.

As women, we have been blessed with the miraculous
ability to give and carry life. Barring any significant circum-
stances, we, for all intents and purposes, are born with the
ability to become mothers. I distinctly remember that, even
as a teenager, I was (what felt) oddly aware of my womb.
Maybe all women are, but it's certainly not something we talk
about. (Is it?)

Fast forward to age twenty-six. I was newly married, and
we were ready to have a baby. All I knew was that it seemed

like the next logical step. We dated, we got engaged, we were married, we had a dog, and now all we needed was a baby! I had picture-perfect images in my head of what pregnancy would look and feel like. I even hid balloons in my shirt to see what I would look like with a cute little baby bump (oh, come on, you've done it too!). And naturally, I figured that getting pregnant would happen quickly and easily. After all, we had decided this was the time, so what could go wrong?

To my surprise, I didn't get pregnant right away, and as you can imagine, I was quite frustrated. Why wasn't this happening the way it was supposed to? What was wrong with us? And even worse, what was wrong with *me*?

All I could think about were the years I spent listening to family, friends, teachers, and doctors telling me how horrible it would be to get pregnant out of wedlock and how I would end up as a teen mom if I so much as looked at a boyfriend with anything less than perfectly pure thoughts. I had escaped such a fate, so now that I was married, I welcomed the missed period, the positive test, and the baby bump to come. So why wasn't it happening?

Then one fateful morning, much to my surprise (and joy!), a magic little line appeared on a pink-and-white stick. In early June 2008, I was elated to discover that I was, in fact, finally pregnant! Now, to put things in perspective, we had only technically been trying for five short months. But for my misinformed, impatient, twenty-six-year-old, ready-to-be-a-mother mind, it had been an eternity.

The day we found out we were going to officially become parents, my husband and I ran to Target and bought two stuffed elephants—one pink and one blue. They were soft and sweet and just waiting to be loved by a precious baby boy or girl. We wanted to give one to each of our mothers, and since we didn't know the sex of our sweet baby just yet, we thought we would give the pink elephant to my mom and the blue to my mother-in-law.

Our parents were beyond excited, as we expected them to be. This child would be my mother's first grandchild and the first in over five years for my mother-in-law, not to mention the first from her eldest son. So were they excited? Yes, to say the least.

All our family and friends seemed to be equally happy for us as well. We spared not a single loved one when sharing our good news; we told everyone! Parents, grandparents, siblings, friends, neighbors, and even the elderly couples at church whom we had grown to love as they always seemed to give us knowing smiles as they rooted for us. We were elated, and we wanted everyone to know. Our baby was finally on his or her way!

I called my doctor's office right away to let them know that I would be joining the ranks of their pregnant patients. They gave me an expected due date based on the information I provided to them and scheduled an exam, as well as an ultrasound. I was thrilled to find out that my baby was due on January 31, 2009, just a couple of weeks past my birthday on the sixteenth. Everything was starting to sink in. This was really happening!

I was a young, healthy woman ready to start a family. I did everything right: took my prenatal vitamins religiously, avoided soft cheeses and cold cuts, and wrote copious notes along the margins of *What to Expect When You're Expecting*. I was pregnant, prepared, and ready for baby. It was such an exciting time!

Nine weeks into my pregnancy, we were scheduled for an ultrasound. The doctor told us the purpose of the procedure was to "date" the baby, claiming they would be measuring the fetus for age as a means of defining a more accurate and exact due date. What they didn't tell me (in so many words) was that an ultrasound at eight to ten weeks is truly to test the viability of the pregnancy. In other words, they want to see if the fetus has a heartbeat.

The nurse called my name, and off I waddled to the quiet, dark room, lit only by the light of the computer screen. The thirty-seven ounces of water that I had to drink prior to the appointment was causing me to have the gait of a nine-months-pregnant woman about to give birth as opposed to the first trimester mommy that I actually was.

When I entered the room, the hum of the ultrasound machine was nearly silent but caused my excitement to bubble.

"Any bleeding with this pregnancy?" The technician was cold and her questions pointed.

"No." Thank God.

"Any morning sickness?"

"Nope." Not yet!

"Weight?"

"Um." I looked at my husband, eyebrows raised. "I'd rather not say," I said with a giggle.

"Weight?"

Man, she was cranky. And as I reluctantly admitted my weight, I thought it might be clear that I had already been eating for two.

I laid back on the table as instructed and lifted my shirt as the technician stuffed an oversized paper bib into the fly of my pants. It wasn't uncomfortable at all, unless you find it odd for a miserable forty-something woman to stick her hands into the elastic of your underwear. She placed the wand on my stomach and slathered the cold gel all over my midsection.

Here we go!

"I'm going to look at some boring stuff first," the tech informed me and my husband as we gripped hands.

"Okay."

Silence. Why isn't she saying anything?

"Is something wrong?" I asked.

The silence became deafening as I stared at the screen, now barely breathing and paralyzed at the thought of what might be coming yet prayed would never come to pass.

"I'm not finding any cardiac activity."

My heart began pounding. Was it enough to make my baby's heartbeat too?

My husband and I stared at the screen as the technician slid the wand over my stomach, back and forth, pressing, clicking away at the machine.

"Do you even *feel* pregnant?"

Excuse me?

I looked up at my husband. His glare was fixed on our baby as if he was trying to give it life through his eyes. His beautiful eyes.

"You can relieve your bladder. I am going to get the doctor, and she will have a word with you."

I slowly rose from the table after wiping the now-fatal gel off my belly. The world seemed to stand still as I stood in simultaneous desperation and numbness. I turned to my husband and fell into his arms. Tears streamed down his face as mine soaked his tie.

"Please, God…please give my baby life!" I cried out to the only One who could change my fate. I cried out to the same God who created our baby miracle to once again prove His power.

My husband rocked me in the coldness of the room as we waited to see the doctor. The doctor arrived. She told us she was sorry, as we would hear countless times from countless people over the next dreadful hours, days, and weeks. They told us that the baby was measuring eight-and-a-half weeks and that her little heart had stopped beating just one short week before the appointment. Just one moment ago, so did mine.

I've always dreaded the word *miscarriage*. I've had visions from as long as I can remember of pregnant women losing baby arms and legs and fingers and toes. I had been told long ago of my grandmother's horrific miscarriage just before she had become pregnant with my mother, and the fear of living through that nightmare had always ailed me.

When we left the doctor's office that day, they handed me a booklet entitled *Understanding Miscarriage*. My worst fear had come true.

How did this happen? What did I do wrong? Did I eat something that I was not supposed to? Did I do something that I was not supposed to do? Why, God? *Why?*

The horrible reality is that one in five pregnancies does not result in the birth of a child but rather in the loss of a small, helpless life. There is no scientific explanation for many of these miscarriages, only the anguish of knowing that "something just wasn't right."

Although I don't have a background in medicine nor the slightest understanding of all that can go wrong, I do know this: for over eight weeks, my baby's heart was beating, and for over eight weeks, her littlest life was the biggest part of mine.

No one ever told me that the faint pink line that signified my baby's life would quickly cause her heart to flatline in less than ten weeks. We prepare for marriage. We prepare for pregnancy. But do we ever prepare for the death of an unborn child? Where was *that* lesson in health class?

As young women, we play with baby dolls and Barbie dolls. We have dreams of becoming the perfect wives and the best mommies. It's all so fantastical and intriguing and then—*bam!* Reality slaps us right across the face.

When I lost that sweet little baby, I once again became acutely aware of my womb. I knew there had been life in there, and suddenly that life was gone. I had gone from feeling so full to instantly feeling completely empty, and it was in those moments that I cried out to God.

No one ever prepared me for the pain, the emptiness, the loss. Nothing will ever take the place of that little angel who grew inside of me for two precious months. No one will ever understand the sorrow that I felt. But I knew there would be life again. And there was.

Liam and Emily

We lost our first child in July 2008 and found out we were expecting once again in October of that same year. Liam Michael was born on June 27, 2009, five days past his due date and making a grand entrance after more than twenty-five hours of labor and nearly three hours of pushing. I swore I might never be able to go through it again—and then came Emily.

While Liam was planned, Emily came along a little sooner than expected. We had just decided to start trying for a second baby, and *bam*! I was pregnant again. I was filled with excitement and prepared for another boy, so when we found out she was a girl, my heart was full and I was happy my dreams of pink and purple, ribbons and curls, tutus and dressing up were about to come true.

Liam had already exceeded my expectations of what being a mommy was all about. He was just about eighteen months when we found out I was pregnant again, and at that young age, he was already charming, energetic, and hilarious. But he was (and still is!) extremely stubborn. In other words, he has been giving me a run for my money since the moment he arrived! And I wouldn't have it any other way.

Emily, while a lot like her brother, is a character all her own. She is a tiny little ball of sass and yet one of the sweetest baby girls you will ever meet. She makes us laugh on a daily basis, adores her big brother, and has brought a new level of joy to our family that we didn't even know was possible.

I love my kids, and I realize I risk sounding like the annoying, obnoxious, photo-showing, braggadocio mom right now, but I'm okay with that. You know why? Because we should all be so blessed to have moms who love us in a way that forces them to nauseate others with their stories, photos, successes, and shortcomings. And if you plan to have children one day (or already do), embrace your obnoxious bragging rights. It means you love your children, and to that, I say, brag on!

Okay, so what's my point? I have many.

First of all, if our first baby hadn't gone to be with the Lord, we would never have had Liam. Of course, I am not saying one child is better than the other, more important or more worthy of living here on earth. But what I am saying is that, for whatever reason, the Lord wanted that first child to be home in Heaven with Him. And He also knew exactly what He was doing when He entrusted us with our sweet baby boy. Liam is a very special child, and I know the Lord has great and mighty things ahead for him. And had we not had Liam when we did, we would not have had Emily either. So you see, everything always works out according to His perfect plan.

My prayer is this: that even in our darkest hours, we remember who He is. Even at our lowest points, we keep our eyes on the cross. And even when all hope seems lost, we never question that His plans are perfect and our lives are His. Because when it is all said and done and when the day draws to a close, it is He who is in complete control.

Someday, I will enter into the gates of Heaven and when I get there—God I pray I get there!—I want to see His face. Then, I want to see hers. My first baby, the little girl the Lord has given me sweet dreams and visions of dancing at His feet, will greet me with a twirl and a sparkle in her eye because He is good, and He has kept her safe in His arms.

I pray I meet you there too.

Daughter of Destiny

She did not consider her destiny; Therefore her collapse was awesome; She had no comforter.

Lamentations 1:9 (NKJV)

How often do we take our own destiny for granted? It feels as if the future is a fairy tale that we will never attain, yet we know—especially as believers—that what our future holds is the promise of God. Believe it or not, He has crafted your destiny, He has written your fairy tale, and He holds you in the palm of His hand. So why don't we trust in *that*? Why don't we stand on that alone as our anticipation for tomorrow?

Why do we take our lives into our own hands?

Lamentations 1:9 tells us of Jerusalem's fall from grace. The city (or "her") is you, it's me, it's us. We are the "she" who so often fail to consider our "destiny," and therefore, our "collapse is awesome." We fall long and hard, and we weep for fear of no one to comfort us. But why?

If only we understood the promises and power of God, we would run with fervor toward the destiny He has so deliberately and delicately designed for us.

When I was nineteen, I was told I would be a writer. I was told—in a powerful prophetic Word from the Lord—that one day I would marry a leader, and I did. Here I am the wife of a good man, a strong man, a man of God who is a leader of men in so many ways. I was also told that one day I would be a voice to a generation, and here I am, writing to you. Here I am, speaking to a generation of young women I have a passion for and a desire to see rise up in ways that move the kingdom of God and this world to levels that have never before been seen. I do not reflect on these things to boast, nor do I wish for you to take from this that I chased after what was spoken over me to make these things come to pass out of my own ambition or desire to do so. Because the truth is, even if I wanted to, I couldn't. I didn't. But He did it all.

The truth is that I have been forever humbled by His grace. I have been blessed beyond measure not thanks to my works but in spite of me. You see, when I received that Word, I was in a deep, dark place. But the Lord still spoke to me. His truth transcends my mistakes.

At the time, I was a freshman in college. I had been struggling with a relationship I had started nearly three years earlier when I was only sixteen. I had been wrapped up with a boy whom I passionately and desperately loved to my own demise. But so goes young love for so many of us. We fall from grace, just as Jerusalem did, and our "collapse is awesome." I made choices I knew I shouldn't have made. I did things, went places, and became a girl I knew I shouldn't have been. Yet I did, and I was.

So here's the question we so often ask of ourselves as pretty Christians and young women who love the Lord: "If I know I shouldn't, then why do I do it still?"

We're told to stay pure. We're told to be righteous. We're told to seek the love of Christ, and the love of the right man will follow. We're told to stand on the Word, and our lives will stay on the straight and narrow. But the truth is, we don't. We compromise, we lose sight of our faith, we seek approval, and we wrap our identity up in what others think and believe to be true about us. We long for the love of a man—sometimes any man—who will notice us, show us just an ounce of appreciation, or, let's face it, even give us negative attention.

Listen, making choices that are less than excellent are not reserved for the heathen down the street or the girl with the short skirt and the plunging neckline who sits across from you in class. We all compromise. Some of us just hide it better than others.

Are there some who don't? Sure. And mostly, our image of them looks something like Laura Ingalls from *Little House on the Prairie*. Accurate or not, that was always my vision of what the perfectly pure Christian woman looked like. And it only made matters worse.

We set unrealistic expectations. We get wrapped up in the laws of the land and preachers on the pulpit. And instead of chasing God's heart, we fall victim to our own. When it comes to purity, we lack the insight into the why and focus too much on the how. We feel like it would be impossible to stay pure and remain faithful to our salvation if we don't wear skirts to our ankles or turtlenecks in muted colors and keep our noses out of *Cosmopolitan* and buried deep in the Word. But that's not purity. That's legalism. That's not righteousness; it's misguided obedience.

No matter what we look like, the clothes we wear, or the goals we set in life, we should remain forever focused on our destiny, and to do that is to chase after God's own heart.

Ladies, don't you want what the Lord has for you? Why settle? Why do we lean on our own understanding to end up in relationships full of pain, devoid of love? Why do so many marriages end in divorce? Why do we compromise all that we are and everything we are called to be in desperate search for a future that is bright when the very way to get there has already been laid out before us?

If and when we think we can do better than God, we end up disjointed, dissatisfied, disappointed, and dejected. And how do I know this? Because I've watched it happen to almost every single woman around me my entire life—and it nearly happened to me.

I can assure you that the guy you think you are nothing without is keeping you from the something you are meant to be. How do I know? Because I have been there. I have felt that incessant longing for the wrong man. I have operated out of emotion that I believed to be love, that I believed would trump the need to be equally yoked with a true man of God, and I have compromised my salvation for the "love" of a human being. I was wrong every time.

See, here's the problem: We convince ourselves that all we need is love. We want love. We need love. We thrive when we feel love. So what do we do? We seek love in every area of our lives. We seek to love and be loved by our family, our friends, our boyfriends, our pets, and even our possessions.

We are obsessed with *feeling* love. Think that's crazy? How many times a day do you check your phone to see if you have a text message? Or how many times do you log into Facebook to see who has "liked" your status or viewed your photos? The actions may vary, but the drive is the same: to find and to feel love.

We are surrounded by the world's definition of love—so much so that we buy into it. And yes, we all buy into it. We see love on television. We are told that love is between a man and a woman, two men, two women, or sometimes between multiple people. We are inundated with images, sounds, and definitions of love that are anything but what love really is. So how do we know when love is real?

If you've ever been to a wedding, you've probably heard 1 Corinthians 13 read aloud:

> Love is patient, love is kind. It does not envy, it does not boast, it is not proud. It does not dishonor others, it is not self-seeking, it is not easily angered, it keeps no record of wrongs. Love does not delight in evil but rejoices with the truth. It always protects, always trusts, always hopes, always perseveres. Love never fails.
>
> 1 Corinthians 13:4–8 (NIV)

My favorite part of this scripture has always been "Love never fails." God clearly defines what love is for us. He wants us to know that if it really is love, it will line up with His word. Now, can we convince ourselves that what we believe to be love does, in fact, fit this definition? Sure. Can you fit a square peg into a round hole? Contrary to popular belief, sometimes you can; if the hole is big enough, almost anything can fall into it.

You can fool others, you can even fool yourself, but you can never fool God.

Take a look at what 1 Corinthians 1:26–31 says about the wisdom of the Lord and being wise when it comes to our calling and purpose in life. The Message translation says this:

> Take a good look, friends, at who you were when you got called into this life. I don't see many of "the brightest and the best" among you, not many influential, not many from high-society families. Isn't it obvious that God deliberately chose men and women that the culture overlooks and exploits and abuses, chose these "nobodies" to expose the hollow pretensions of the "somebodies"? That makes it quite clear that none of you can get by with blowing your own horn before God. Everything that we have—right thinking and right living, a clean slate and a fresh start—comes from God by way of Jesus Christ. That's why we have the saying, "If you're going to blow a horn, blow a trumpet for God."

> 1 Corinthians 1:26–31

In other words, it's all about Him. It doesn't matter what anyone thinks or says about us. It doesn't matter what we think or say about ourselves. All that matters is that He has chosen each and every one of us to do great and mighty things if only we will let Him work in our lives.

Here is what we need to know and I mean really *know* deep down in our spirits:

We are nothing without Him, but with Him, we are something.

I want you to read that again. Say it out loud:

We are nothing without Him, but with Him, we are something.

Can you grasp that? Can you really read that and understand what it means? Because as a young woman, I thought I knew this. I thought I had this concept down, but I didn't. In fact, I still don't. To this very day, I am still unsure that I truly understand what it means to be nothing without Him. And why? Because I never am.

You are nothing without Him.

He is always with you.

Therefore, you are something in Christ.

You are something. You are not just a number. You are not just a name. You are a beautiful something with a purpose, a destiny, and a future in God. You are a multifaceted something that has depth, undeniable potential, and promises of blessings beyond your wildest dreams. You are not a mistake. You are not an accident. You are not alone, and you are not forgotten. You are not unwanted. You are not unworthy. But you are *nothing* without Him.

Once you take a hold of that, your life will change. Your relationships will change because you will turn from believing you are nothing without him—whoever "him" might be at the moment—and realize you are only nothing without Him.

You are more than a pretty face.

You are more than just a *pretty* Christian.

You are a daughter of destiny. And you are not alone.

> And let the beauty of the Lord our God be upon us,
> And establish the work of our hands for us;
> Yes, establish the work of our hands.
>
> Psalm 90:17 (NKJV)